TO KNOW HIM

Felix Alexander

American Literary Press, Inc.
Five Star Special Edition
Baltimore, Maryland

To Know Him

Library of Congress
Cataloging in Publication Data
ISBN 1-56167-828-7

Library of Congress Card Catalog Number:
2003110387

Published by

American Literary Press, Inc.
Five Star Special Edition
8019 Belair Road, Suite 10
Baltimore, Maryland 21236

Manufactured in the United States of America

This book is dedicated to my daughters, Latavia Shante and Jasmin Mone for their love, support and encouragement.

To My Daughters: Latavia and Jasmin,

You are a gift from God. Therefore, I thank Him for you each day. You both have brought an abundance of joy in my life. From the time of your birth up to the present time, I have not stopped praying for you.

Your smiles, warmth and love daily bring joy and happiness to me. I can't imagine what my life would be like if God had not blessed your mother and I with the two of you. I pray that I will always be the kind of father that God desires me to be. I will always strive to be a positive role model, teaching you to observe, obey and fulfill God's commandments.

Regardless of what situations or circumstances you find yourselves in, please know that you can always come to me. I will listen attentively and carefully to every word. My response will always be in accordance with God's Word.

Thank you for believing in me and supporting my writing. I love you both with my whole heart. I thank God for each of you.

I pray that you will continue to "Follow me, as I follow Christ".

Your Loving Dad,
Felix

TO KNOW HIM

There is a void inside of me
That is longing to be filled
But riches, houses nor worldly fame
Can't come close to paying the bill.
Even being consumed with passionate love
Doesn't satisfy or quench my thirst
Because I hunger to know Christ,
That's why He must be first.

My greatest desire is to know Him
To know the richness of His love,
To know the sufficiency of His grace
And the peace that comes from above.
Thus, I'm determined not to conform
To anything contrary to God's design
But I'm willing to be transformed
By the renewing of my mind

I am willing to lay aside
Everything that hinders me
I am willing to deny myself,
Take up my cross and follow thee.
Thus I turn and face the world
Committed to Christ and not to them
Thus I freely surrender all
Just to know, to know Him

Philippians 3:10 "That I may know Him and the power
of His resurrection, and the fellowship of his sufferings,
being made conformable unto his death;"

TABLE OF CONTENT

ENCOURAGEMENT

Beyond the Gift   2
Continue to Trust   3
Don't Forfeit Your Blessing   4
Don't Stop Working   5
Do What Is Right   6
Endure the Storms   8
Fret Not My Child   10
Give It To God   11
Give Something Back   12
Guard Your Heart   14
Help Us Forget   15
In God's Time   16
It's All Very Possible   18
Live It   20
Live By God's word   21
Look In The Mirror   22
Open Your Eyes   23
Put On The Armor   24
Renew Your Mind   26
Seek Me First   28
Stay With God   30
Stick With Love   31
Study God's Word   32
Subdue Those Thoughts   33
Take Control   34
Trust In God   35
You're There Because   36

SALVATION

Allow Me	38
A New Beginning	39
He Knew	41
Help Me, Dear Lord	42
He Will Tell You	44
In My Life	46
It Takes God	48
It's Our Choice	50
It's Up To You	51
Jesus, My Lord, Savior and Friend	52
Take A Minute	54
Thank You Jesus	55
The Challenges of Life	57
This Thing	58
We're Not Alone	61
When Will We Learn	62

TRUTH

A Child of the King	64
Bedtime	65
Christians	66
Deny, Take Up and Follow	67
Do We Really Expect	69
Everyone Need's a Friend	70
Faith	71
God, I'm Ready	72
Heaven	74
Hindrances From Within	75
I Can Get Back Up	77
I Love Him More	78
It Takes Faith	79

Love Is Blind   80
Pruning Is Necessary   82
Remember To Pray   83
Something Within   84
Struggles   86
Under Construction   88
We Can't Go Back   89
We've Been Called   90
Whatever We Do   91
What Is It   92
You Where Chosen   94

WORSHIP & PRAISE

Be Ready   97
He'll Make It All Right   98
Here I Am Lord   99
Jesus, King of Kings   100
Lord, I Need You   101
Lord, I   102
Lord, I'm Willing   103
Lord, You're The One   104
Nobody, But You Lord   106
Rest In the Lord   107
Step   108

ENCOURAGEMENT

Joshua 1:8 "This book of law shall not depart out of thy mouth; but thou shalt meditate therein day and night, that thou mayest observe to do according to all that is written therein: for then thou shalt make thy way prosperous, and then thou shalt have good success."

Psalms 1:1 "BLESSED IS the man that walketh not in the counsel of the ungodly, nor standeth in the way of sinners, nor sitteth in the seat of the scornful."

Proverbs 4:7 "Wisdom is the principal thing; therefore get wisdom: and with all thy getting get understanding."

2 Timothy 3:16 "All scripture is given by inspiration of God, and is profitable for doctrine, for reproof, for correction, for instruction in righteousness;"

2 Timothy 3:17 "That the man of God may be perfect, thoroughly furnished unto all good works."

BEYOND THE GIFT

When you receive a precious gift,
Especially from someone that you admire,
Whether it's a gift you've longed for
Or one you have always desired,
Do not allow your new gift
To reverse what you should do.
It's the giver, not the gift
That has brought this joy to you.

For many a souls, it's the gift
And not the giver that they adore;
Showering praises on the gift,
While treating the giver like before.
Learn to look beyond the gift
To the one from whom it came.
Without a giver, there is no gift
And everything will remain the same.

So before embracing your precious gift,
Thank the giver for quenching your thirst.
Acknowledge his sacrifice and his love,
Let him know that he is first.
He will sense your genuine love,
Not your attention when it shifts.
He'll be filled with unspeakable joy,
Knowing you looked beyond the gift.

Ephesians 2:8 "For by grace are ye saved through faith; and that not of yourselves; it is the gift of God."

CONTINUE TO TRUST

When your world seems quite dim
And everyone's questioning whatever you say,
Don't get discouraged and lose hope,
Continue to trust in the way.

When life's issues are pressing you,
Causing you daily to go through.
Resist the temptation to give in,
Continue to trust in what's true.

Although dark clouds appear in the sky,
The sun is still shining bright.
Despite the disappearance of the day,
Continue to trust in the light.

Nothing you now nor will ever face
Can over power our Father above.
Stand your ground and press ahead,
Continue to trust in God's love.

Proverbs 3:5 "Trust in the Lord with all thine heart and
lean not to thine own understanding."

DON'T FORFEIT YOUR BLESSINGS

Despite what the world has to offer,
Regardless of what is promised you.
Don't forfeit your blessings; don't cast them aside,
Stand your ground; to God be true.

Despite how alluring it may be
Or how wonderfully it makes you feel,
Satan's primary and ultimate purpose
Is to kill, destroy and steal.

He will use every method or means
To make you believe there's no way out.
He will lie, cheat and confuse.
His greatest weapons are deception and doubt.

Thus I beseech and even beg,
That you not yield to temptation.
Yielding will delay or forfeit your blessings,
Causing both pain and much irritation.

Don't forfeit your blessings; don't give in;
Keep the faith; stand your ground.
Hold firm to what God promised you.
Don't let Satan bring you down.

Matthew 16:26 "For what is a man profited, if he shall gain the whole world, and lose his soul? or what shall a man give in exchange for his soul?"

DON'T STOP WORKING

Situations develop or circumstances arise,
Which often hinders or disrupts our walk.
If that's not bad, to make matters worse,
People come together to gossip or talk.
Instead of allowing our worldly problems
To wear us down and drain our cup,
We should turn them over to Jesus
And He will keep us filled up.

When nothing seems to be changing,
After we have given our best,
Don't get weary in well doing
And the Lord will give us rest.
When people start putting us down
In hopes of starting a fight,
Don't stop working; endure the abuse
And the Lord will make it right.

When we're depressed or need a hand,
But family and friends walk away.
Don't stop working; keep the faith
And the Lord will lead the way.
No matter what happens in life
That frustrates me or hinders you,
Don't stop working, but press ahead;
And the Lord will bring us through.

Galatians 6:9 "And let us not be weary in well doing; for in due season we shall reap, if we faint not."

DO WHAT'S RIGHT

Death is something we don't like,
But it is what we must face.
When life is over, God will judge
How we ran our earthly race.

If nothing else, it should be said,
We tried to do what is right.
Regardless of what came our way
We lived by faith, not by sight.

This is what should be said,
About our parents, family and friends
No matter what came their way,
They did what was right until the end.

It didn't matter the need nor purpose
They did what was right to do.
Not for show or selfish reasons
They only wanted to make it through.

And when we are called home
Our message should remain strong
We always strive to do what's right
Even when encouraged to do wrong.

Then when our work is done,
A gift will be waiting for me and you;
A home prepared in Heaven above
For everyone, that made it through.

If nothing else, take from this
That death will call our name
Therefore we should do what's right
And avoid the pit of sin and shame.

It's our choice to do what's right
Or face whatever comes our way.
If we're wise, we'll do what's right
And not be surprised come judgment day.

Colossians 3:23 "And whatsoever ye do, do it heartily as to the Lord, and not unto men."

ENDURE THE STORMS

Storms seem to appear out of nowhere.
Bringing with them wind and rain.
They also disappear as quickly as they came,
Leaving behind destruction and pain.

Like the storms that appear on land,
We have similar storms in our life.
They are just as destructive,
Bringing with them trouble and strife.

They come when we least expect,
Disrupting those things which weren't put away
People not anchored are easily uprooted,
While others are broken and led astray;

Unless we're committed to stand for something,
We will fall for almost anything.
We'll be caught up and carried away,
Because we accept what whomever bring.

To endure the storm, the wind, and rain,
We must be rooted and grounded in love.
We must be established in the faith
And practicing the doctrines of God above

We must have rock solid faith,
One that's built on a firm foundation;
Therefore when the storm clouds rise,
We'll not experience fear or frustration.

No matter how fierce the storm,
Our anchor will hold to the rock.
We may bend, but not break,
We'll never be separated from God's flock

Ephesians 4:14 "That we henceforth be no more children, tossed to and fro, and carried about with every wind of doctrine, by the sleight of men, and cunning craftiness, whereby they lie in wait to deceive."

FRET NOT MY CHILD

When you've done your very best,
Yet others continue to criticize you.
When you've gone that extra mile
Just to ensure you make it through

When you endure insults and abuse
Even from those whom you share,
When you've given your all and all,
But no one seems to really care.

Fret not my child I know your heart
I'll be there, just do your part.

Because I know what's in your heart,
Rest assure I'm here for you.
So don't you worry or even fret
I'll make sure you make it through.

Be not deceived by what you see
For things are not as they appear
I AM GOD; I'M in control
There's no reason to fret or fear.

Fret not my child I know your heart
I'll be there, just do your part.

Psalms 37:1 "FRET NOT thyself because of evildoers,
neither be envious against the workers of iniquity."

GIVE IT TO GOD

Feelings of anger, feelings of guilt,
Feeling as though you can't go through.
Sad and lonely or feeling blue
Worried about problems or just what to do.
Despite what you are feeling
Or what's bothering you
Give it to God
He'll bring you through.

Rejected by friends, hated by others,
Misunderstood by people, confused by things,
Unsure of yourself, afraid of the unknown;
Questioning and wondering what tomorrow will bring.
Despite what you are feeling
Or what's bothering you
Give it to God
He'll bring you through.

Regardless of circumstances, doubts and fears,
Regardless how long, you've traveled this road.
Give it to God He cares for you,
He'll bare your burdens; He'll lighten your load.
Despite what you are feeling
Or what's bothering you
Give it to God
He'll bring you through.

1 Peter 5:7 " Casting all your cares upon him; for he careth for you."

GIVE SOMETHING BACK

When much is given, much is required.
Because we're expected to share with others
Although we think we don't have much,
We have far more than our brothers;

Thus we are our brother's keeper,
If we don't help no one will.
Their circular path will continue,
Unless given a chance to earn a skill.

There are times people don't care
And there are times, when they do.
But those that do, normally don't have
The resources needed to help them through.

Every adult living on the street
Isn't there because they want to be.
Few are equipped with the means
That will allow them to be free.

How many children actually choose
To live the life, they currently live?
Due to their parent's economic condition,
They only have what others give.

That's why we should lend a hand
To those hungry or sleeping in sacks;
We've been blessed; we're doing well;
Isn't it time we give something back?

Give what you can, whatever you have,
Do what ever you can do.
Please just give; give something back
This could have been either me or you.

Psalms 84:11 "For the Lord God is a sun and shield: the Lord will give grace and glory: no good thing will he withhold from them that walk uprightly."

GUARD YOUR HEART

Be not taken
By kind words,

Be not deceived
By lovely gifts,

Be not fooled,
By your emotions,

Guard your heart,
Keep it secure.

Hide God's word
In your heart;

Keep it rooted
And grounded in love.

Give it wisdom,
Feed it knowledge.

Guard your heart,
Keep it pure.

Proverbs 4:23 "Keep thy heart with all diligence; for out of it are the issues of life."

HELP US FORGET

Things we've said, things we've done
Have brought about some difficult days.
Some brought heartaches; some brought pain;
However, we haven't changed our ways.
They've hindered progress, created a stand still,
And brought back skeletons from by-gone years.
Can't we forget, can't we let go?
Must we continue shedding tears?

Help, I pray; show us the way
Forget the past and move ahead.
Help us press, to strive towards
The reason Christ was once dead
Help us forget, lest we continue
To climb up yesterday's hill.
Help us forget, lest we fail
To press towards God's Holy will.

Help us forget, that we lay aside
Weights and sin that hold us down
Help us forget, lest we fail
To some day wear the victor's crown.
Help us forget what happen before,
Give us the faith to run our race.
Help us forget the wrong we've done,
By focusing on God's Amazing Grace.

Philippians 3:13 "Brethen, I count not myself to have apprehended: but one thing I do, forgetting those things which are behind, and reaching forth unto those things which are before."

IN GOD'S TIME

There is a time for all things
In heaven above and earth below
But if they're done the wrong time,
They will not help us grow.

Regardless of what we may desire,
We shouldn't rush or move too fast.
Fulfilling those desires may make us happy,
But that instant joy will not last.

It may only last for a moment;
Probably providing an emotional high
When that feeling is past and gone,
We may barely just get by.

When we fail to do things
In the time that God declares,
Though it appears we are prospering,
We actually have much more to bear.

Listen my friend, there's always a blessing
When things are done in God's time.
If we wait for His approval,
They will not cost a dime.

When they're done in our time,
The price we pay isn't worth the cost.
We'll not only lose material things,
Our very soul could be lost!

There's nothing in life that's worth having,
If we must disobey or commit a crime;
But everything in life is a blessing,
When it's done in God's time.

In God's time, all is well
He makes sure we get our rest.
In God's time, everything is good
Because He knows what is best.

Ecclesiastes 3:1 "To every thing there is a season, and a time to every purpose under the heaven."

IT'S ALL VERY POSSIBLE

There are treasures to behold,
There are wonders to see,
And they're all very possible
For God holds the key.

The things you like to do,
The places you like to go;
It's all very possible,
If to God you don't say, No

The fame you wish to obtain,
The goals you wish to achieve,
It's all very possible
If in God you trust and believe

The friendships you wish to keep,
The people you wish to meet,
It's all very possible
If to God you speak and greet

The hate you wish to remove,
The love you wish to share,
It's all very possible
If you stay in God's care.

The fears you wish to loose,
The courage you wish to gain,
It's all very possible
If to God you go and remain

The wisdom you wish to have,
The things you wish to know,
It's all very possible
If you allow God's love to flow.

The life you wish to live,
The people you wish to love,
It's all very possible
If your strength comes from above

The roads you travel maybe rough
And storm winds may blow.
But it's all very possible,
If you turn to the God I know.

Matthew 19:26 "But Jesus beheld them, and said unto them, With men this is impossible; but with God all things are possible."

LIVE IT

We're constantly reminded to do the right thing,
Regardless of the situation that we face
It's talked about and taught daily
In almost every conceivable place
It's good that we remind one another
To always do the right thing;
But it's better to live it,
Then we could testify about what it brings.
Instead of merely talking and teaching,
It should be our daily walk.
The best way for us to share
Is to live and walk what we talk.
Live the way that we should,
Doing whatever is good and right:
Live it regardless of the situation
Because it will come to light

Living it helps to reinforce
Whatever we ask others to do.
It also shows how living it
Can help them make it through.
If we expect others to live right,
We should practice what we preach
If we aren't willing to live it,
We're wasting time when we teach
People do what ever they see,
Rather than what we ask them to do.
Thus, we should live it everyday,
So others will see and follow through.

James 1:22 "But be doers of the word, and not hearers only, deceiving your own selves."

LIVE BY GOD'S WORD

There are those who quote scripture
As if they wrote, the words they speak.
Each word gently flows from their lips
Like strength draining from the weak.
Scriptures flow one after the other
Like they were once suppressed:
Always providing a sound statement
To whatever issue is being addressed.

This is truly a gift from God,
Correctly quoting His Holy Word.
Reciting knowledge that you've gained
From what you read or may have heard.
This is certainly an admirable trait,
One that we should strive to emulate
The only issue with quoting Scripture
Is not living by what you dictate.

If you quote it, strive to live it,
Otherwise your message is misleading.
What goes in should come out,
Or we're lying, robbing and stealing.
What goes in doesn't defile man,
But what he allows to come out.
When we live by God's word,
We walk in light and don't cast doubt.

2 Corinthians 5:7 "(For we walk by faith and not by sight:)"

LOOK IN THE MIRROR

Look in the mirror; who do you see,
The person you are or hope to be?
The reflection has a direct impact,
It dictates the manner in which you behave.

If you see the person that you are,
Then your vision is somewhat blurred.
Unless it helps you come to grips
With the mess that you have made

Even if you see a wonderful person,
Who's that person striving to be?
For we should always strive to become
The person God ordained us to be.

Strive to see that special someone
God has called and set apart.
Although there are rough edges today,
God can mold you into a work of art.

If you don't see him or her now,
Keep on looking, believing His word,
One day you'll see, you'll finally know
That God is true to His word.

1 Corinthians 13:12 "For now we see through a glass, darkly; but then face to face; now I know in part; but then shall I know even as also I am known."

OPEN YOUR EYES

There are times when what we see
Is not what it appears to be;
Either your focus is not clear,
Or your eyes maybe deceiving thee.
Whatever the reason, whatever the cause
You need to know what's really there.
Open your eyes so you will know
Who, what, why, when and where;

Open your eyes; take a look around
Know who is being misled.
Open your eyes to power and greed
Learn what really is being said.
Open your eyes to the world
Know why you are going through.
Open your eyes to the truth
Then you'll know what to do.

Open your eyes; read God's word
And you will know where not to go.
You will learn how to live
And what's required for you to grow.
Open your eyes; take a stand,
Or you may never, if ever see;
Everything that God has actually prepared
And set aside especially for thee.

Psalms 119:18 "Open thou mine eyes, that I may behold
wondrous things out of thy law."

PUT ON THE ARMOUR

The negative things that we encounter
Appear to be caused by man.
But they are the works of Satan,
Disguised to conceal his evil plan.

This is why many don't realize
That we're in a fatal fight;
It's not a battle between two people,
It's a spiritual war between wrong and right.

To win this war, we must be prepared
To endure it until the end;
That is why we should wear,
A force that protects and always defends;

Something that makes us strong in the Lord
And in the power of His might.
Something that will keep us safe
Against the forces of the night

We don't wrestle against flesh and blood,
But against wickedness in high places;
That is why we must put on,
A Force that will help us keep pace.

Put on the armor, the armor of God.
It will protect us on the roads we trod.

Something that will make us strong;
Ready to with stand in the evil day.
Something that will keep us standing
After we've given in every way.

Lets gird up our loins with the truth
That we maybe able to stand;
Strap on the breastplate of righteousness
To protect us from Satan's clan;

Shod our feet with the gospel
In preparation to face each day;
And take up the shield of faith
To quench the darts that come our way.

Put on the helmet of salvation
To protect us as we trod.
And take the sword of the spirit,
Which is the word of God.

Then through prayer and supplication
Make our requests to God be known.
By watching daily with perseverance,
We'll be blessed from His throne.

Put on the armor, the armor of God.
It will protect us on the roads we trod.

Ephesians 6:11 "Put on the whole armour of God, that ye may be able to stand against the wiles of the devil."

RENEWING OUR MIND

Offering our bodies as living sacrifices,
Holy and pleasing to God above;
Thinking of ourselves as we should,
Exercising good judgment and sharing His love;

Not conforming to this world,
But being transformed by renewing our mind.
Living our lives in a way,
That God considers perfect and kind.

Developing the gift freely given us,
Using it wisely to bring relief.
Fulfilling our calling as unto God,
Applying it freely to promote belief.

Hating what's evil, clinging to what's good;
Being kindly affectionate in God's love.
Joyful in hope, patient in affliction,
Faithful in prayer while sharing His love;

Singing with singers, mourning with mourners,
Blessing the persecutor, not cursing our brother.
Not being conceited and not proud,
But living in harmony with one another.

Refusing to repay evil for evil,
Doing what's right in God's eyes.
Living in peace, taking no revenge
Inserting the truth where they're lies.

Feeding our enemy, giving them a drink,
Showing God's love, as we should.
Not being overcome by evil's snare,
But overcoming evil with our good;

This is what renewing our mind
Means to us who live for Christ;
Because we know what it took
When Jesus paid that awesome price.

Romans 12:2 "And be not conformed to this world, but be ye transformed by the renewing of your mind that ye may prove what is that good, and acceptable and perfect will of God."

SEEK ME FIRST

Since inviting Jesus into my life,
There were times when I questioned Him.
Times when problems were weighing me down
Because I wasn't listening, I was following them.

Thus I was not able to stand.
I was actually about to give in
So, I asked Jesus, what was wrong?
Why was I being beaten by sin?

I said things I should not have,
I didn't know I was going astray.
I thought you would always be there,
Why have you turned and walked away?

God replied, my dear child,
I haven't turned or walked away.
I am the same, yesterday and today
And tomorrow I'll be the same way.

It was not I it was you
That decided to relinquish his crown.
You allowed the world's pleasure
To entice you and bring you down;

However, if you just repent,
I'll be pleased to accept you back.
I will cleanse and make you whole,
And place you on the right track.

Although your sins are as scarlet,
I'll make you white as snow.
I will cast them in the sea
And no one will ever know.

I am God, your Heavenly Father,
I will always be here for you.
Regardless of what you're going through,
Seek me first; I'll bear it for you.

Matthew 6:33 "But seek ye first the kingdom of God and
his righteousness; and all these things shall be added unto
you."

STAY WITH GOD

Though some prosper from doing wrong,
Be not deceived, God's not mocked.
What man sows, he shall reap,
Including those things done in the dark.

So don't conform to the world's ways,
It's not real it's by design.
Strive instead to walk by faith,
Be transformed; renew your mind.

Then when the darts and arrows fly,
They will not come near thee.
The Armor of God will allow you
To boldly stand, firm and free.

But if you stumble or even fall,
Don't allow it to hinder your walk.
Quickly repent and confess your sin,
Take a stand and walk your talk.

Stay with God; He'll bring you through
He'll direct your steps and guide you.
There is nothing He'll not do
Just so you can make it through.

Galatians 3:1 "O Foolish Galatians, who hath bewitched you, that ye should not obey the truth, before whose eyes Jesus Christ hath been evidently set forth, crucified among you?"

STICK WITH LOVE

In our wide and wonderful world,
We find both hate and love.
Hate is often a result of ignorance,
And love comes from God above.

God is the essence of love,
He's the reason we're here today.
As long as we stick with love,
We will never be led astray.

If we hate, that which is good,
We won't endure the struggles of life.
We will stumble and eventually fall
Because hate generates sin and strife

Therefore we should not hate.
It's a burden that's hard to bear.
Unlike love, it'll weigh us down;
Withholding what we have to share.

When you're facing something bad,
Shun hate and stick with love,
Love will ensure, that we live
With our Father in Heaven above

1 John 4:16 "And we have known and believed the love
that God hath to us. God is love; and he that dwelleth in
love dwelleth in God, and God in him."

STUDY GOD'S WORD

Study God's Word, you will learn
How the world came to be?
How long it took, what was first
And what's commanded of you and me?
Study God's Word; experience God's love
That freely flows from His Grace.
The Agape Love that God avails
And gives to all in the race.

Study God's Word; discover the key
To free yourself from sin and strife;
Unlock the knowledge to the mysteries
Of hope, salvation and eternal life.
Study God's Word; improve your knowledge
About the occurrences of yesterday;
Embrace the understanding and the meaning,
Learn of tomorrow and of today.

Study God's Word; search the scriptures'
In them you'll find a heavenly treasure.
An abundance of wisdom is yours to have,
Designed to subdue our worldly pleasures.
Study God's Word to help you gain
Whatever in life you hope to acquire.
It provides a path and directs the way
Doing whatever is your heart's desire.

2 Timothy 2:15 "Study to show thyself approved unto God, a workman that needeth not be ashamed, rightly dividing the word of truth."

SUBDUE THOSE THOUGHTS

There are times when contrary things
That will occasionally cross our mind.
Instead of thinking as we ought,
We think thoughts that we should bind.

We must learn to subdue those thoughts,
To suppress and lay them aside;
To take them captive when they appear
Or find our selves in sin and pride.

We must subdue every thought
That either blocks or hinders our race.
We must maintain control of our mind,
If we're going to grow in grace

Subdue those thoughts that cause us
To lust for that which should not be;
Subdue the ones that make us crave
Things that entangle you and me;

If our thoughts bring no peace,
Give no praise nor share love.
Subdue those thoughts when they appear,
They're not from our Father above.

2 Corinthians 10:5 " Casting down imaginations, and
every high thing that exalteth itself against the knowledge
of God, and bringing into captivity every thought to the
obedience of Christ."

TAKE CONTROL

Take a moment; give some thought
To the things that you do
Are you pleased with all the things,
That you are going through?

Is there something, you don't like?
Then take the time, make it right.
You may not like the way it feels,
But it'll help you sleep at night.

Make a decision and hold firm,
Don't turn back after you've begun.
Plot your course, steady your pace,
And focus on Jesus as you run.

Make up your mind; stop wasting time.
Life gets tougher day-by-day.
Take control, make the call.
Don't wait until tomorrow, do it today.

Embrace your emotions; tackle your thoughts;
Fire your feelings and strangle strife.
Now is the time; today is the day
To take control and reclaim your life.

Hebrews 12:2 "Looking unto Jesus the author and
finisher of our faith; who for the joy that was set before
him endured the cross, despising the shame, and is set
down at the right hand of the throne of God."

TRUST IN GOD

Hard it may appear to be,
There is nothing you can't do.
Especially when you trust in God
And obey all that He tells you.

It matters not what you think,
What you feel or even see.
What really matters is God's word
And what He promised you and me.

Don't get discouraged and give up;
Please don't question and don't doubt.
Learn to trust and acknowledge God,
Because He is, The Way out.

Thus I encourage you to stand,
Trust and believe in God's word.
Do only what He commands you,
Don't be swayed by what is heard.

Things are not as they seem
And the battle isn't ours to fight.
We must learn to trust in Him,
And walk by faith, not by sight.

Psalms 37:3 "Trust in the LORD, and do good; so shalt thou dwell in the land, and verily thou shalt be fed."

YOU'RE THERE BECAUSE

Although your job isn't what you desire
You have a mission, which is to inspire.
It's your job and your task
To get people to remove their mask

You've been appointed and placed in there
To let them know, they're going nowhere
You're there to share God's grace from above
By being a witness and a vessel of love

You're there to share a kind word,
Which maybe something they haven't heard
You're there to encourage those who are down
Not to give up, but to press for a crown.

You are there to share a smile
Even if you must walk a mile
You're there to do whatever you can
To encourage them to take God's hand

Although the mission will get rough;
Keep the faith; you must be tough
And when it appears, you're climbing a hill
Remember you're there because it's God's will

Ephesians 4:16 "From whom the whole body fitly joined together and compacted by that which every joint supplieth, according to the effectual working in the measure of every part, maketh increase of the body unto the edifying of itself in love."

SALVATION

John 3:3   "Jesus answered and said unto him, Verily, verily, I say unto thee, Except a man be born again, he cannot see the kingdom of God."

John 3:5   "Jesus answered, Verily, verily, I say unto thee, Except a man be born of water and of the Spirit, he cannot enter into the kingdom of God."

John 3:7   "Marvel not that I said unto thee, Ye must be born again."

John 3:16   "For God so loved the world, that he gave his only begotten Son, that whosoever believeth in him should not perish, but have everlasting life."

Romans 10:9   "That if thou shalt confess with thy mouth the Lord Jesus, and shall believe in thine heart that God hath raised him from the dead, thou shalt be saved.

Romans 10:10   "For with the heart man believeth unto righteousness; and with the mouth confession is made unto salvation.

ALLOW ME

Allow me to be your friend,
One whom you trust and depend
Allow me to hold your hand,
As you travel through this land.

Allow me to share your task
To prevent you from wearing a mask
Allow me to keep you strong
Whether you're right or you're wrong.

Allow me to ease your pain,
Whether it's dark or it rains.
Allow me to lead the way
To prevent you from going astray

Allow me to do all things
That joy, peace and happiness brings.
Then give me your life and love,
I'm your father in heaven above.

Revelations 3:20 "Behold, I stand at the door, and knock:
if any man hear my voice, and open the door, I will come
in to him, and will sup with him, and he with me."

A NEW BEGINNING

When things happen we least expect
We often ask Lord why me?
What have I done or even said?
What can I do to get free?

While enduring the heartaches and the pain,
We sometimes experience guilt and shame.
We take ourselves through several changes
From self-denial to self-blame;

Our inner feelings create problems
Like anger, depression and loneliness.
Instead of helping, we complicate matters.
We get discouraged and experience stress.

These occurrences are going to happen,
They come regardless of what we do.
Although we're seldom prepared for them,
We should be able to always go through.

Learn to address them as they come,
Acknowledge and accept what's done or said.
Then give yourself a little time,
Collect your thoughts and press ahead.

39

Develop a plan and take action,
Confess what's written in God's word.
Surround yourself with credible others
And learn to repeat what is heard.

Remove yourself from the past,
And gain a new perspective on life.
Renew your mind; change your thinking
Don't be troubled by sin or strife.

Doing these things will not free us
From those things that bring us down;
But they are a new beginning,
A sure way to gain your crown.

Isaiah 43:19 "Behold, I will do a new thing; now it shall spring forth; shall ye not know it? I will even make a way in the wilderness, and rivers in the desert."

HE KNEW

When God decided to send Jesus
To bridge the gap between Him and man,
Jesus was told, He was aware,
That He was required to take a stand.

Aware of the task, He freely came
Ready and willing to accept the blame.
He had to come in such a way,
His message would promote His name.

Thus God sent Him as a child
To experience life as we do.
Enduring the same type of trials
To prove we can make it through.

He knew what things awaited Him,
He knew the hardships of the race
He knew the pressures and the pain
And the people He would face.

He even knew that He would die,
Because He is the chosen one;
Knowing all this, He still came
He knew God's will had to be done.

Luke 2:49 "And he said unto them, How is it that ye
sought me? Wist ye not that I must be about my Father's
business?"

41

HELP ME, DEAR LORD

Lord, change my head, my mind and my heart;
Change me Lord; take me apart.
Lord, I'm tired of living this way,
Help me dear Lord, please do it today.

There are days when I first rise
I give you praise for opening my eyes.
Lord, I thank you for my life,
I even thank you while going through strife.

Yet there are days when I go astray.
I'm moved by whatever comes my way.
Although I know it's not your will,
I find myself consumed with it still.

Lord, I'm tired of this bumpy ride,
Thus, I'm ready to let go my pride.
Lord, I'm ready to be true
To the promise I made to you.

Here I am extending my hand,
I'm relinquishing all, I'm taking a stand.
Shunning the world and clinging to thee,
Lord, You're the one, the one for me.

Do what you must, but break me down;
I need my life to be turned around.
I am ready and willing to do
Whatever it takes to bring me through.

Lord, change my head, my mind and my heart;
Change me Lord; take me apart.
Lord, I'm tired of living this way,
Help me dear Lord, please do it today.

Hebrews 4:16 "Let us therefore come boldly unto the throne of grace, that we may obtain mercy, and find grace to help in time of need."

HE WILL TELL YOU

The world's crisis is at your door,
Impatiently waiting to get in
Bringing with it an extensive list
Of those it enticed to commit sin.
It allured people of all races.
Many who believed, they were secure;
Even those who lived in peace and comfort
Have fallen away and can't endure.

Men, who once, where in-charge
Were convinced to let things slide.
Even women, who rose to fame,
Welcomed the crisis and let it ride.
The crisis took them by surprise,
They didn't think; they could be beat.
Many are now either in jail
Or without a home and nothing to eat
Those who are affected the most
Are being consumed by drugs and drinking.
They are freely engaging in sex,
Not realizing how fast they're sinking.

The crisis is seducing, pulling them away,
Filling their lives with fear and doubt.
It was able to make them believe,
There's no hope, no way out.
The crisis somehow tricked them all,
Disguising itself as something nice.
Then when they were least expecting,
It levied on them a costly price.

It stripped them of their freedom of choice
And replaced it with a heavy load.
It's all because they weren't willing
To travel the straight and narrow road
Now it's knocking at your door
With a special story just for you.
Do you let it in or turn it away?
What are you going to do?

How do you plan to face the crisis?
Do you have someone to help you through?
Where will you turn for an answer?
What are you going to do?
You can't ignore it or run away,
You must answer, you must decide.
Whatever you do, consult the Lord
Seek Him out; swallow your pride.
If you're seeking the right answer
Or wondering how to make it through,
Turn to God; trust in Him;
He will tell you what to do.

He'll tell you how to handle,
Not only the crisis, but all you face.
He'll give you what is needed
To help you run and win your race.
He'll be there whenever you need Him,
No matter what you're going through.
Stop what you're doing and go to Him,
He will tell you what to do.

Proverbs 3:6 "In all thy ways acknowledge him and He shall direct thy paths."

IN MY LIFE

Late one night, I woke up
Sweating and trembling because of a dream;
It was so real, so very clear,
I woke up and started to scream.

I dreamed that I was left alone.
Force to handle my life myself.
Left to deal with my problems,
No guarantee of wealth or health.

Because I knew I wasn't able
To handle what I was going through.
I got down and earnestly prayed,
I asked God to what to do.

He agreed to take control,
When I gave my life to him.
He came in, made me promise
Not to live my life like them.

God assured me, if I confessed,
Repented and believed in His name.
He would cleanse me with His blood
And completely remove all my shame.

I would be saved by His grace
And I would inherit eternal life.
He promise to make me whole
And cleanse me from all sin and my strife.

He also said, He'll be there,
He'll never leave or forsake me.
No matter what I'm going through
Know that He has set me free.

That same night, I accepted Christ
As Lord and Savior of my life;
Since that night, I sleep well,
Knowing He is in my life.

Hebrews 13:5 "Let your conversation be without
covetousness; and be content with such things as ye have:
for he hath said, I will never leave thee, nor forsake thee."

IT TAKES GOD

Challenged by circumstances, consumed with fear,
Questioning and wondering what tomorrow will bring.
Devastated by problems, weakened by guilt,
Reluctant to face just one more thing;

Imprisoned by rage, manipulated by hate,
Hindered from answering your heavenly call,
Stripped by deception, raped by innocence,
Done quite simply to make you fall.

Enticed by money, swindled by kindness,
Filling you with resentment and doubt.
Abandoned by family, criticized by friends,
Leaving you alone, hopeless and without.

Tortured by lust, imprisoned by greed,
Causing your mind to go without rest.
Tormented by passion, mesmerized by beauty,
Distorting what truly is the best.

Life unfortunately isn't always fair,
Things seldom occur as we expect.
Forcing upon us additional pressures,
Causing us to question what we should reject.

How can we escape this ferocious fate?
What will it take to let it past?
While man will say, it takes money,
The truth is, it will not last.

I have learned that it takes God,
To overcome what you're going through.
God's the answer, the only way,
He has to fulfill the call in you.

Through God and His Love,
You can conquer all your fears.
Instead of planning or seeking revenge
Let God wipe away your tears.

His Love will give you strength,
Humble your pride and eradicate hate.
Quench the fire of physical lust;
He'll help you find the perfect mate.

He'll subdue your anger, ease your burdens,
Give you peace that you can enjoy.
What does it take to make this happen?
It takes God and His joy.

Philippians 4:7 "And the peace of God, which passeth all understanding, shall keep your hearts and minds through Christ Jesus."

IT'S OUR CHOICE

God has shaped and molded us
To be the person He wants us to be.
He also gave each of us
A special gift that was free.

The only request of you and me;
Let Him be Lord of our life.
When we do, He will deliver,
Removing our heartaches, pain, and strife.

He will not make any demands,
He wants us to freely choose.
But He has told each of us,
If we reject Him, we will loose.

Considering this, it's our choice,
We must decide to run this race.
We can choose to run it alone
Or to rely on God's Grace.

Whatever way we decide to go,
It's our choice; we hold the key.
God has placed it in our hand,
It's our choice, what will it be?

Joshua 24:15 "And if it seem evil unto you to serve the Lord, choose you this day whom ye will serve; whether the gods which your fathers served that were on the other side of the flood, or the gods of the Amorites, in whose land ye dwell: but as for me and my house, we will serve the Lord."

IT'S UP TO YOU

Your life comes with many opportunities,
It's your decision to follow through.
Whether you respond or do nothing,
Whatever happens is up to you.
It's up to you to make a difference
In every aspect of your life;
Only you can truly decide
Whether to endure or eliminate strife;
You can't continue blaming others
For the things that happen to you;
You must assume the responsibility,
You're accountable for what happens to you.
Instead of sitting on the sideline of life
Get off the bench and get in the game.
As long as you are giving your all,
There's no reason to be ashamed.

However, if you are merely watching
And waiting for others to do their thing,
You deserve what comes your way,
Whatever the situation or circumstances bring.
Now is the time to make up your mind,
To follow through with your plan;
Write your goals; commit yourself,
And tell yourself that you can.
As long as you put God first
There's no limit to what you can do.
You can be or do what you will,
There's no limit, it's up to you.

Habakkuk 2:2 "And the Lord answered me, and said, Write the vision, and make it plain upon tables, that he may run that readeth it."

JESUS MY LORD, SAVIOR, AND FRIEND

All my life, I've been searching
For someone to be my friend;
Some one who I can trust,
One whose friendship knows no end

Through the years, I've come to know
Several people who came close,
But none of them ever became
The type of friend I needed the most.

Some of the friendships last a little while,
Usually ending for one reason or another.
Either one of us would move away
Or get upset with the other.

Things are said and feelings are hurt,
Making it tough to make amends.
As time goes on, we pull away,
Suddenly we are no longer friends.

This situation occurs again and again,
Causing me to consider just giving up.
But my thirst wouldn't let me quit,
I was determined to fill my cup.

After repeatedly struggling with this thing,
I finally decided to face my fear.
That's the day, when I discovered,
A friend has always been standing near.

He had been patiently waiting,
Hoping to be a part of my life.
He extended his hand and softly said,
Let me remove your sin and strife.

I opened my heart and allowed Him
To be my Savior, Lord, and Friend;
He didn't hesitate, not for a moment,
But quickly and quietly moved right in.

What a change, He's made in my life.
I'm so happy and full of joy.
There is nothing, nothing more exciting,
Than having a friend that I enjoy;

He's a friend who doesn't allow
Time or distance to get in the way;
He always emphasizes the here and now;
Forgetting what happened on yesterday.

He's a Friend, who's always there,
Whether I'm sick or in good health;
He's so loving and oh so kind;
He's more precious than even wealth.

This is the friendship I've longed for,
One I know will never end.
Because this friendship is with Jesus,
My Lord, my Savior, and my Friend.

Proverbs 18:24   "A man that hath friends must show himself friendly: and there is a friend that sticketh closer than a brother."

TAKE A MINUTE

There are things in your life
That keep you from getting ahead.
They encourage you to find fault
Or make excuses for what is said.
What will it take to help you handle
The things that you go through;
What does it take to help you understand?
That these things are hindering you?

Daily encouragement may help develop
And also strengthen your positive side.
Learning the experiences of one another,
May help you overcome your pride.
But it will take something more
To free you from your mental cell;
It will take a Spiritual encounter,
That frees you from a burning hell.

Acquiring money and managing it
Will improve your financial lot,
But nothing but the love of Jesus
Can get you out of this spot.
Take a minute be born again,
It will remove all sin and strife.
It is quick and very easy.
Take a minute, change your life!

John 3:7 "Marvel not that I said unto thee, ye must be born again."

THANK YOU JESUS

There was a time when I used to feel
Having you in my life was no big deal.
I could live, however I choose,
Everything to gain; nothing to lose;

As I traveled, I sinned with ease,
Taking life for granted, doing as I pleased.
There's no doubt if you came then,
I would've been lost because of sin.

While I was doing all I could do,
You interceded and brought me through.
Thank you Jesus, now I know,
I need you everywhere I go.

Now I can talk about your love,
I can share my joy from above.
I can share with my friends
That your love knows no end;

With a song in my heart
And a smile on my face,
I'll tell people wherever I go
About your love and your grace.

Thank you Jesus for obeying God
And for showing me which road to trod.
Thank you Lord for lending an ear,
Thanks for teaching me not to fear.

Thanks for answering my prayers with care
And for sharing the burdens I bare.
Thanks for sharing and for caring
And thanks for not being overbearing.

Thank you Jesus for coming as a man
And for fulfilling the master's plan.
Thank you for loving and for living,
Thanks for teaching the value in giving.

Thank you for dying on the cross
So our souls would not be lost.
Thank you for not staying down,
Thanks for rising to wear your crown.

Psalms 118:1 "O Give thanks unto the Lord; for he is good, because his mercy endureth for ever."

THE CHALLENGES OF LIFE

As we journey through this life,
Many things challenge us to sin.
Whether its love, happiness or peace,
We must learn not to give in.

Challenges can come from family and friends,
Bringing with them a desire to win.
While others come from those we meet,
But the greatest ones come from within.

The challenges to do what is right,
When the world is doing wrong;
The challenges to just say no,
When the world is going along.

When we're faced with these challenges
They come with struggles and strife.
To win this battle and the war,
We must accept Christ in our life.

Christ will help us face each challenge,
Even if it is our husband or wife;
He alone is willing and able
To help us win the challenges of life.

Ephesians 5:6 "Let no man deceive you with vain words: for because of these things cometh the wrath of God upon the children of disobedience."

THIS THING

Throughout my life, I've always tried
To do things my own way
I never allowed any one or thing
To dictate what I do or say

I did whatever I wanted to do,
Whenever I wanted to do it.
It didn't matter the time of day,
If I wanted to, I did it.

All I cared about was having fun,
In whatever way that I could;
It was my way of dealing with pain
Instead of responding like I should.

If someone said something, I didn't like
I was quick to tell them where to go.
It didn't matter who they were,
There wasn't a punch I wouldn't throw.

There were people who would tell me
I could be free of strife.
But I would simply tell them,
Nothing was better than living my life.

But deep inside, that wasn't true,
I was tired of living that way.
I was hungry and empty inside,
But I wasn't able to walk away.

58

Then one day, my eyes were opened
To this precious and wonderful thing;
This thing came in, changed my life,
And gave me a song to sing!

This thing opened doors once closed,
And told me things I never knew.
It also taught and gave me respect,
Not just for myself, but for others too.

This thing changed the way I talk,
The way I walk, and the way I look.
It made me feel oh so good,
It took me off the hook.

It reached down, picked me up
And told me what I need to do.
It now gives me encouragement
In whatever I'm going through.

This thing teaches me how to live,
How to face each and every test.
It teaches me to laugh in a crisis
And cry when I'm doing my best.

It teaches me not to strike back
When someone intentionally does me wrong,
And to always lend a hand;
Helping those who are not strong.

This thing is wonderful; it's so sweet,
There is nothing that can compare.
It's better than the greatest thing,
That this world has to share.

It's very unique and oh so precious,
More precious than diamonds or gold;
It's everything I need or want
It's so wonderful just to behold.

This thing has really changed me,
It turned my life right side up.
All that was missing in my life
Is overflowing in my cup.

It's joyous, peaceful and filled with love
There's nothing like it, it's so fine.
This thing is wonderful, it's so real;
This thing is JESUS and He is mine.

Acts 1:8 "But ye shall receive power, after that the Holy Ghost is come upon you; and ye shall be witnesses unto me both in Jerusalem, and in all Judaea, and in Samaria, and unto the uttermost part of the earth."

WE'RE NOT ALONE

There are times we feel alone,
Like when asked to hold the phone.
Or when we're in a strange land,
And no one seems to understand.
We're not alone and never will be
Jesus is watching over you and me.
We may feel alone in a crowd,
While people are shouting or talking loud.

Or when we are the only one
That disagrees with what others call fun.
We're not alone, don't think we are
Jesus has others who aren't very far.
There are many on this road,
That allows Jesus to bare their load,
They no longer fret or worry,
They don't even get in a hurry.

They have learned, give it to Christ.
He has paid the ultimate price.
When we invited Jesus in our heart,
He promised never to leave or depart.
In His own time, He will fulfill
All of our needs if we do his will.
We will never, ever be alone,
As long as Jesus, remains on our throne.

1 Samuel 12:22 "For the LORD will not forsake his
people for his great name's sake; because it hath pleased
the LORD to make you his people."

WHEN WILL WE LEARN

Lord, You provided a map to follow,
We chose a path that is shallow.
Lord, You agreed to lead the way,
But we chose to go astray.
When will we learn your path is clear?
When will we learn, that Jesus is near?
Lord, You provided what we need to know,
Instead we chose not to grow.

Lord, You provided a comforting guide,
But we chose to keep our pride.
When will we learn your word is true?
When will we learn there's comfort in you?
Lord, You provided a guiding light,
But we chose the darkness of night
Lord, You provided everlasting life,
But we chose Satan as our wife.

When will we learn to not let Satan in?
When will we learn with him we can't win?
When will we learn to stop giving in
To weights and measures that causes us to sin
When will we learn not to follow the pack,
If we're to keep Satan off our back
When will we learn to keep in stride?
We must have JESUS as our guide.

Psalms 127:1 "EXCEPT THE LORD build the house,
they labour in vain that build it: except the LORD keep
the city, the watchman waketh but in vain."

TRUTH

Proverbs 23:23   "Buy the truth, and sell it not; also wisdom, and instruction, and understanding."

John 8:32   "And ye shall know the truth, and the truth shall make you free."

John 14:6   "Jesus saith unto him, I am the way, the truth and the life, no man cometh unto the Father, but by me."

John 16:13   "Howbeit when he, the Spirit of truth, is come, he will guide you into all truth: for he shall not speak of himself; but whatsoever he shall hear, that shall he speak : and he will show you things to come."

A CHILD OF THE KING

It is good to sometimes get
The little things that we expect;
But we must realize that life is tough,
And getting things are sometimes rough.
Even those things that appear free,
Often may cause us to flee.
However, there is one great thing
That certain behavior will surely bring.
It's a behavior that indicates change,
One that the world thinks is strange.
One where Christ is Lord of all,
Whether you're sitting or standing tall.
With Him there are no mistakes;
You know exactly what it takes.

You never wonder what's awaiting you,
Regardless of what you choose to do.
Why not surrender your life to God,
Let Him protect you from the rod.
He will save you by His grace,
He'll help you run this Christian race.
Just stay committed and follow through
And no surprises will overtake you.
Because God has made it clear
What He considers near and dear.
Give your life to Jesus Christ,
He has paid the eternal price.
Be not consumed with worldly things,
Because you are, a Child of the King.

Ephesians 5:8 "For ye were sometimes darkness, but now are ye light in the Lord: walk as children of light."

BEDTIME

Each of us must one day
Come to our earthly end;
It will be like going to bed,
And not getting up in this life again.
Where we get up is determined
By how we live from day-to-day,
Whether we live for the world
Or walk the straight and narrow way.
If we live for the world,
We'll get up in a burning hell.
But if we live for Jesus Christ,
When we get up, all will be well.
Since we don't know the day or the hour
Or when it will be our bedtime,
Thus we should always be ready
And it will not cost us a dime.

Let's stop saying and even doing
Those things contrary to God's will,
Let us listen that we may learn
Whether to move or just be still;
Although we think we have time
We don't know what tomorrow will bring,
We don't know and can't imagine
When the bell for us will ring.
Just remember when it's bedtime
It's too late to make things right.
Thus we should live for Christ each day,
And avoid being cast out of his sight.

Hebrews 9:27 "And as it is appointed unto men once to die, but after this the judgment."

CHRISTIANS

Christians we are I'm pleased to say;
Worshipping God in a special way.
Humbly confessing our many sins;
Opening our hearts for Jesus to come in.
Providing our services for the comfort of others.
Hoping to promote harmony among our brothers.
Faithfully serving our father above,
While willingly sharing his amazing love

Prayerfully bowing down on our knees,
And asking him to fulfill our needs.
Joyfully singing to the glory of God,
As we walk the roads he trod.
When challenged by Satan, we quicken our pace,
Determined not to fall, but to stay in the race.
As children of God, we're standing tall,
Ready and willing to give him our all;

When we resist whatever is wrong,
God will surely keep us strong.
Diligently working and giving our best,
Patiently waiting to take our rest.
Trusting that Jesus takes our hand,
Joyfully leading us to the promise land.
That is our proof, we worked not in vain,
All our struggles were worth the pain.

1 Peter 2:9 "But ye are a chosen generation, a royal priesthood, an holy nation, a peculiar people; that ye should show forth the praises of him who hath called you out of darkness into his marvellous light."

DENY, TAKE-UP AND FOLLOW

Why do we think, we can live this way,
Get what we want and not have to pay?
Why do we believe, we can have it all
Without working, struggling or taking a fall?
Why do we spend time devising a plan
That gives us life without lifting a hand?
Why do we desire a crown for a cross
But are not willing to pay the cost?
There's a cross that we must bear,
If we desire, a crown to wear.

We must realize, we must learn
To face our challenges and take our turn.
To receive a crown, we must enter the race,
And carry our cross with a consistent pace.
Although it's tough, it can be won
By looking to God while we run.
To run this race, we must decide
Who to trust and always abide.
It can be long and demand a lot,
But run whether we like it or not.

There are three things we must do,
Just so we can make it through.
We must deny, take-up and follow
Or we'll end up lost and hollow.
We must deny and humbly submit
And to His statutes we must commit.
We must deny, forsake our life,
If we're to become His dear wife;
We must deny, forego cheap thrills
And yield our members to God's will.

We must deny and lay aside
All selfish desires and earthly pride
While denying ourselves, let us pray,
Take up our cross; carry it each day.
Take up our cross; face our trials,
Believing one day we'll only have smiles.
Take up our cross; endure tribulation,
Believing one day we'll have a celebration.
Take up our cross; endure the pain,
Believing our faith is not in vain.

After denying, taking up each day,
We must follow Jesus; do things His way.
We must follow Jesus, plant His seeds
And also water, but as He leads.
We must follow Jesus, put Him first,
Seek His kingdom and after righteousness thirst.
We must follow Jesus, spread His word,
And baptize or teach those who haven't heard.

When all is said, when all is done,
We would have run as well as won.
When it's over and Satan's bowing down,
We will receive a golden crown.
But only if we deny selfish pride,
Take up our cross and follow God's guide.
By denying ourselves, taking up our cross
And following Jesus, we'll not be lost.

Matthew 16:24 "Then said Jesus unto his disciples, If any man will come after me, let him deny himself, and take up his cross and follow me."

DO WE REALLY EXPECT

Many of us are quick to blame
Others for our sin and shame
We find fault in what is true,
Especially when we don't make it through.

We make excuses when things go wrong,
Knowing full well where blame belongs.
We put down family and friends,
When we don't achieve our desired ends.

We have the nerve to even say,
God knows our heart, it'll be okay.
Do we really expect family or friends
To take the blame for all our sins?

Do we really expect what is true
To justify failures for me and you?
Do we really expect to pass any test
By making excuses for our mess?

Do we really expect to someday win
By putting down others again and again?
Do we really expect God to say,
I know your heart it is okay?

Certainly we know, God is true,
He does the same for me and you.
We are responsible; we will pay;
Thus we should, do it God's way.

Galatians 6:7 "Be not deceived, God is not mocked, for whatsoever a man soweth, that shall he also reap."

EVERYONE NEED'S A FRIEND

There are times when things go wrong,
There are things we can't mend.
There are times when words won't do,
That is when, we need a friend.

There are moments when no one cares,
There are moments when we can't pretend,
There are moments when no one understands,
That is when we need a friend.

Everyone needs a friend,
That's what makes the world go round.
Someone you can always call
And tell what's bringing you down.

Everyone needs a friend;
It's what makes life worth while.
Sharing the joys and the sorrows,
Willing to go the extra mile.

Everyone needs a friend;
It's the epitome of true love.
It's a relationship like no other;
Designed and developed by God above

Proverbs 18:24 "A man that hath friends must show
himself friendly; and there is a friend that sticketh closer
than a brother."

FAITH

Faith is the substance of things hoped for
It's the evidence of things not seen
Faith is the key that unlocks tomorrow,
It's the truth we should glean.

Faith is the step we take in the night
The move we make by God's grace.
Faith is trusting, what we don't see,
And allowing God to dictate our pace.

Faith is acting on an inner belief,
That guides and directs the path to take.
It is believing the Spirit of God
Will always tell you the move to make.

Walking by faith is done with ease,
When we surrender to His call.
Thus faith hinges on one thing,
We must give God, our all and all.

Hebrews 11:1 "Now, Faith is the substance of things hoped for, the evidence of things not seen."

GOD I'M READY

God when I came to you,
I was wretched and quite undone.
I had no hope, no peace within,
I had nothing and no one.

God when I first met you,
You changed my life from within.
You touched my heart, healed my body,
And cleansed me from all my sin.

You gave me a new start
And delivered me from all harm.
You taught me what to do,
You even held me in your arms.

You removed me from where I was
And showed me which way to go.
You even provided me a guide,
Someone to ask, what I didn't know.

You blessed me in so many ways,
All of which, I didn't deserve;
You freely gave your love to me
And all you ask is that I serve.

But to serve, I must be willing
To die daily to selfish desires;
Because I can't come after you
In my present state and attire;

I must be willing to be broken
To release that which hinders me,
I must surrender to your will
To escape that which imprisoned me.

Once I'm broken, I can be given
To the people you've called me.
I can then be also sent
So I can help set others free.

God, I'm ready to be broken
Ready to obey your every command.
I am ready to totally submit
And ready also to take a stand.

Give me Lord to the people
That you destined just for me.
Lord my will is completely surrendered
And all of me is hid in thee.

Let me go; let me run;
Lord, the race, that you begun.
Now I know, it's not my will,
But thy will that must be done.

Matthew 26:42 "He went away again the second time, and prayed saying, O my Father, if this cup may not pass away from me, except I drink it, thy will be done."

HEAVEN

Heaven is an attainable goal.
It's not easy, but it's ours to behold.

We must repent; confess our sins;
Give Christ our life and be born again.

We must deny self; take up our cross;
And follow Jesus or our soul will be lost.

Trust in God; continue to pray;
Acknowledge Him daily or we'll go astray.

Step out on faith; take a stand;
Against anything that hinders God's plan.

Walk in truth and in love,
Looking to Jesus and God above.

Fatigue will come, but don't give in,
Stay in the race; go for the win.

The road gets roughs, especially at night.
But His yoke is easy; His burdens are light.

Let the Holy Spirit be our guide,
We'll get to Heaven; we'll be by His side.

Philippians 4:13 "I can do all things through Christ
which strengtheneth me."

HINDRANCES WITHIN

Hindrances come in different ways,
With a unique color, shape, and size.
Yet they share the same goal,
Keeping us all from the prize.

Most hindrances are from without
But there are some from within.
They're the ones that we seldom
Believe or see as vessels of sin.

They are usually the little things
That we handle almost every day;
Some are people that we know
Others are those with whom we play.

It is difficult to consider
Someone who is very near
To be the source of our pain,
A force that, we should fear.

But the hindrances from within
Can be burdens that we bear.
They go untouched and often unnoticed,
We handled them with love and care.

They disrupt our daily walk,
Constantly creating turmoil and trouble.
Although the results don't appear bad,
The time invested is usually double.

They create work; generate problems;
And leave us feeling hurt and abused.
They take away our energy and time,
Leaving us tired and often confused.

Until we learn to accept the truth
And see these hindrances as they are,
We may continue promoting peace
But we will not get very far.

Face the hindrances; don't run away;
Know that they cause us to sin.
Address the issue; give it to God;
Let Him remove the hindrances within.

Romans 7:21 "I find then a law, that, when I would do good, evil is present with me."

I CAN GET BACK UP

Although life's situations have knocked me down,
I refuse to let them hold me back.
I'm getting up with renewed confidence.
I'm determined to stay in the pack.

Dusting myself off, I'm pressing ahead,
Focused and committed to moving along;
No longer will they get in my way,
I'm determined to get where I belong.

I will fully develop the gift
That almighty God has given to me.
I will discover the primary reason
He has called and set me free.

Despite the fact, once I'm up,
These situations may come up again.
But I'm determined to press ahead,
No longer will I be entangled by sin.

Should I stumble or get knocked down,
I will not relinquish my cup.
God has promised and assured me,
That I can get back up.

Proverbs 24:16 "For a just man falleth seven times, and
riseth up again, but the wicked shall fall into mischief."

I LOVE HIM MORE

The world is like a blossomed rose,
A delight to see, a pleasure to hold;
Giving the appearance of a precious metal,
But it isn't silver or gold.
What the world has to offer
Causes a struggle in you and me.
Creating a battle between good and evil,
And preventing us from being free;

In the world, there's no peace
Only a pull that's very demanding;
But in God, there is peace,
One that surpasses all understanding.
In the world, there is a feeling
That makes us question where we belong.
But in the Lord, there's a joy
That enables us to be strong.

Even the love of the world,
Wants to always be in control.
But the Love of Almighty God
Has the power to save our soul.
The world can be O so appealing,
Presenting a pleasure behind each door.
Even if it's good, it's not God
And the truth is I Love Him More.

1 John 2:15 "Love not the world, neither the things that are in the world. If any man love the world, the love of the Father is not in him."

IT TAKES FAITH

Faith is the substance of things hoped for,
It's the evidence of things not seen.
We need faith in every thing
Like a baby when he is weane,
It takes faith to be obedient,
Especially when life is taking you through.
Like when you should pay your tithes,
Instead of paying a bill that's due.

It takes faith to stand firm,
When the world says you can't win.
It takes faith to walk away,
Instead of yielding and committing sin.
It takes faith to be courageous
When speaking against that which is wrong.
Whether it's things on your job
Or situations where you don't belong;

It takes faith to trust and believe,
Especially when you can't see your way.
Whether it's a challenge or a test,
Not knowing what may happen today.
It takes faith to live this life,
Walking daily in truth and love.
But it doesn't take just any faith,
It takes faith in God above.

Hebrews 11:6 " But without faith it is impossible to
please him: for he that cometh to God must believe that
he is, and that he is a rewarder of them that diligently
seek him."

LOVE IS BLIND

Love is forgiving, forgetting the past.
Love is pure, perfect, and kind.
Love is accepting, overlooking faults,
Never passing judgment, because it's blind.

Love is blind, but it's fair.
It will survey what's in the heart.
It carefully examines and wisely chooses,
Things that keep us from falling apart;

Love will endure; it'll never give in,
It will stay strong until the end.

Love is blind; it sees no color.
It accepts everyone; it doesn't discriminate.
It precisely perceives the inner man,
While shunning evil and highlighting hate.

Love isn't foolish; it's very wise.
It's opened to all; it's not confined.
It doesn't deceive, it does pretend,
It is receptive and very refine.

Love is blind; this is true,
But it will never mislead you.

Love is blind to wealth and fame;
It is blind to pain and strife.
Blind to today and tomorrow,
But it's sees into our life.

Love is compassionate, considerate and honest.
It's unlike anything we'll ever find.
It's understanding, kindhearted, and true.
Love is Jesus; He's God's design.

Love is blind; this is true,
Love is God, through and through.

1 Corinthians 13:13 "And now abideth faith, hope and charity, these three; but the greatest of these is charity."

PRUNING IS NECESSARY

Trees are pruned to stimulate growth
By cutting away excessive waste.
Pruning eliminates needless branches
And adds to the overall taste.
Trees produce more when they're pruned,
When those branches are cut away.
Clearing the way for new growth
And a larger lot come harvest day.
Just like trees must be pruned,
We must also prune our life.
We must remove or cut away sin,
Freeing our selves of trouble and strife.
But unlike the pruning of a tree,
Which involves a physical cutting away,
Pruning our life is actually spiritual,
It requires that we fast and pray.

Although pruning, can be painful,
It is necessary for us to grow.
Without it, we go astray
And fail to share what we know.
Through pruning, we can subdue
The worldly things that keep us down;
Freeing us to press ahead
And one day receive our golden crown.
In both cases, we must remove
That which doesn't allow fruits to bear.
But the results of pruning our lives
Produces more for us to share.

Leviticus 25:3 "Six years thou shalt sow thy field, and six years thou shalt prune thy vineyard, and gather in the fruit thereof."

REMEMBER TO PRAY

Thoughts of yesterday flood my mind,
Taking me back to the past.
Days when we were covered with sin
And life was moving oh so fast.

Although those days are past and gone
We should always remember to pray.
To give thanks and petition God
To bless us each and every day;

Thus I pause to say a prayer
For God to anoint and set us apart;
To open our eyes and enlighten us
To renew our mind and our heart;

God, our Father, our Creator and King
Please Dear Lord by your grace,
Lengthen our love; strengthen our faith
And bless us with a larger place.

A place where we trust in you
And not in what we now possess.
A place where you are Lord
One where we can be at rest;

This we ask and humbly pray
In the name of Jesus Christ,
And we give thanks to you O God,
You let Jesus pay our price.

1 Thessalonians 5:17 "Pray without ceasing."

SOMETHING WITHIN

There are times when little things
Seem to get the best of me.
They cause me to do or say
Things that hinder God in me

But in the mist of my actions,
I find myself feeling bad.
Because there is something within
That doesn't like making others sad

Something within that makes me cry,
Even when there is nothing wrong.
Something within that gives me strength,
Even when I don't feel strong

There are days when I feel
Like the world is on my shoulder.
And everything is pressing me down
With the force of a boulder

But then somehow I find myself
Slowly rising from the ground.
As if my problem had only weighed
Nothing more than a pound

Something within that makes me cry,
Even when there is nothing wrong.
Something within that gives me strength
Even when I don't feel strong

84

There are people who seem to enjoy
Trying to drive me up a hill.
They are constantly doing things
To make me go against God's will.

It's very hard to sometimes resist
And I find myself giving in.
But whenever I decide to yield,
I'm convicted by something within.

Something within that reveals to me
What to do and which way to go.
Something within that shares with me
Every thing that I need to know

Whatever the problem, whatever the care,
No matter what I'm going through
There's always something, something within
That knows just what I need to do.

It's not just strictly for me,
It can also be within you.
If you ask and sincerely pray,
Something within can help you too.

Something within that reveals to you
What to do and which way to go.
Something within that shares with you
Every thing that you need to know

1 John 4:4 "Ye are of God, little children, and have
overcome them: because greater is he that is in you, than
he that is in the world."

STRUGGLES

As long as we live, we'll face struggles
From almost every facet of life,
Some will lend to peace and love,
While others generate pain and strife.

The key to facing any struggle
Is preparing for the fight.
We must be properly equipped
Or we'll not last through the night.

The best way to face any struggle
Is to surrender to Jesus Christ.
For He conquered the ultimate struggle,
Giving His life, He paid the price.

Through His death, He provided the way
To overcome struggles that we face.
He gave us His whole armor,
As well as His Amazing grace;

As long as we put on the armor,
With the helmet firmly secure,
We can use His sword and shield,
Face each struggle and always endure.

We must realize there are no struggles
Which were designed by the human race.
We wrestle not against flesh and blood,
But against powers in a higher place

Despite the struggles that we endure,
God is able to set us free.
If we cast our burdens on Him,
He will fight for you and me.

1 Corinthians 10:13 "There hath no temptation has taken you but such as is common to man: but God is faithful, who will not suffer you to be tempted above that ye are able; but will with the temptation also make a way to escape, that ye may be able to bear it."

UNDER CONSTRUCTION

Be not alarmed by what you see
The foundation is laid; the work has begun.
God is molding and shaping me,
But there's still much work to be done.
God has me under construction,
He's preparing me to do His will.
He's using my faults, habits, and ways
To teach me how to be strong and still
Occasionally the words I choose to speak,
Do not come forth in a Godly way.
Do not excuse my poor behavior,
Let me know, but also pray.
Sometimes I act like the world,
Choosing not to acknowledge God.
Tell me about it; give it to the Lord,
Don't admonish me with your measuring rod.

If I should boast or lose control,
It is okay for you to share.
But don't be little nor put me down,
Tell it to Jesus, He'll make me aware.
Whether failing to speak the truth in love
Or not giving thanks in all things,
God does get my attention
Through the trials my actions bring.
During those times when my behavior,
Does not set well with you,
Just remember, I'm under construction,
And God will eventually bring me through.

Matthew 26:41 "Watch and pray, that ye enter not into temptation; the spirit indeed is willing, but the flesh is weak."

WE CAN'T GO BACK TO YESTERDAY

Time ill spent is time lost!
We can't go back to yesterday.
Not for an hour or even a minute,
The time is lost; it's gone away.

We must face what has occurred.
Once it happens done, it can't be undone.
It may be corrected; it may be changed,
But it doesn't erase what was done.

We must be wise when taking an action.
Even if it only costs a dime;
It is permanent, it did occur,
Once it's done, it's recorded in time.

Nothing we do; nothing we say.
Can change the fact, it happened one day.
We can go forward; we can correct,
But we can't go back to yesterday.

Philippians 3:14 "I press toward the mark for the prize
of the high calling of God in Christ Jesus."

WE'VE BEEN CALLED

Let's set aside our selfish desires
And examine the reason we're in this life.
We've been called to be servants,
Not to bring pain and strife.
Although we may touch a heart,
As well as stir the emotions of others,
We've been called to be a friend,
Not to hinder our sisters and brothers.

Thus we must focus on the task
That God has given us to do.
We've been called to be servants,
Ordained to help others make it through.
Let's be committed to our call,
So we don't cause someone to die.
Let's go forth sharing God's word,
Encouraging the world to freely comply.

Let's lay aside our selfish desires,
And learn how to just say no.
We've been called to be ambassadors,
Given a mission and a place to go.
Thus we must change our actions,
We must do what God requires.
We've been called to His messengers,
Sharing and teaching what He desires.

Isaiah 43:1 BUT NOW thus saith the Lord that
created thee, O Jacob, and he that formed thee, O
Israel, Fear not: for I have redeemed thee, I have
called thee by thy name; thou art mine."

WHATEVER WE DO

Each of us is very unique
Made and molded in a special way.
We all have a different method
To face what we encounter each day.

You may cry when you're upset,
While I may scream and shout.
Although we share similar feelings,
We're unique in getting them out

Despite the fact, we are unique,
Our ultimate goal may be the same.
Whether we cry, scream, or shout,
Depends on how we play the game.

How we act, what we say
And even what we're going through
Is neither significant or as important
As honoring God in whatever we do.

It doesn't matter what, when, or where
Nor why or who carries the rod.
Just remember whatever we do,
Let's do it for the Glory of God.

Colossians 3:17 "And whatsoever ye do in word
or deed, do all in the name of the Lord Jesus,
giving thanks to God and the Father by him."

WHAT IS IT?

There is something that we see
That makes us respond a certain way.
Whether its good or it's bad,
We do not turn it away.

Some people often lose control,
Because they can't handle this thing
They don't understand and can't explain
The type behavior this thing brings.

Lots of people even give up,
Because they're tired of playing this game
No matter what they try to do,
Everything seems to remain the same.

What is it that causes us
To act differently than we do?
What is it that takes control,
Directing the changes we go through?

What is it that doesn't care?
What it does or even says?
It is only concerned about itself,
Which is to have its' own way.

I don't know what it is,
But it must be from within.
It's like Satan has taken control,
Dictating how and when to sin

The only way to control this thing
Is with God's power and might.
By His grace and through His love,
We can challenge and win this fight.

Whatever it is, we can repent
And surrender our life to Jesus Christ,
Then we can stand on God's word,
Because Jesus has paid the price.

Romans 12:21 "Be not overcome of evil, but overcome evil with good."

YOU WERE CHOSEN

Out of the darkness, out of the night,
God is bringing men to the light.
Many are being called by the rock,
But you were chosen to shepherd this flock.

You were chosen to take the lead,
To cultivate the soil and plant the seed;
You were chosen to sound the alarm,
As a watchman does to prevent harm;

You were chosen to preach God's word,
Whether or not it wants to be heard.
You were chosen to baptize and teach,
Every one you can possibly reach.

You were chosen to show true love,
The kind, that comes from God above.
You were chosen to do God's will
Whether down in a valley or up on a hill.

God realizes your calling is tough
He realizes the going gets rough.
He also realizes you can't make it alone,
That's why you're not on your own.

He left the Holy Spirit to be a guide,
A caring comforter by your side;
With the power, that He brings
You can deal with all things.

Whatever happens, wherever you trod,
Remember you were chosen and anointed by God.
You were chosen and given the key,
Use God's word to set men free.

Jeremiah 1:5 "Before I formed thee in the belly I knew thee; and before thou camest forth out of the womb I sanctified thee, and I ordained thee a prophet unto the nations."

PRAISE & WORSHIP

1 Chronicles 16:29 "Give unto the Lord the glory due unto his name: bring an offering, and come before him: worship the LORD in the beauty of holiness."

Psalms 9:1 "I WILL praise thee, O LORD, with my whole heart; I will show forth all thy marvellous works."

Psalms 150:6 "Let every thing that hath breath praise the LORD; Praise ye the LORD."

Matthew 4:10 "Then saith Jesus unto him, Get thee hence, Satan: for it is written, Thou shalt worship the Lord thy God, and him only shalt thou serve."

Revelations 22:9 "Then saith he unto me, See thou do it not: for I am thy fellowservant, and of thy brethen the prophets, and of them which keep the sayings of this book: worship God."

BE READY

No man knows the day or hour
When the Lord shall come again.
That is why we must be ready,
Ready and waiting to enter in.
This is truly the only way
To inherit the gift of eternal life
It's the way to get the tools
Necessary to face trouble and strife;
Then, we can prepare for all
That we encounter day-to-day.
That's how we will be ready
To face whatever comes our way.
I want to be ready; got to be ready,
Ready when Jesus comes;

Without a commitment to Jesus Christ,
We'll not be ready when He returns.
Nor will we be able to stop
That final fate of receiving burns;
To be ready for Christ's return
We must be born again.
Committed to living a sanctified life,
Full of faith; free of sin;
This is the only way
For us to be forever free.
This will get and keep us ready,
Until Christ comes for you and me
I must be ready, got to be ready,
Ready when Jesus comes.

Matthew 24:44 "Therefore be ye also ready: for in such an hour as ye think not the Son of man cometh."

HE'LL MAKE IT ALRIGHT

Sick or suffering

Despair or depression

Panic or pain

Chaos or confusion;

Whatever your heartaches,

Your worries or cares

Give it to God,

Your burdens He'll bare,

His yoke is easy,

His burden is light;

He'll walk with you,

He'll make it all right.

Psalms 55:22 "Cast thy burdens upon the Lord, and he shall sustain thee: he shall never suffer the righteous to be moved.

HERE I AM LORD

Unsure of the task
And what you require
But here I am Lord
For whatever you desire.
Going to the world,
Extending a hand,
Speaking against sin,
I'm taking a stand.

I'm ready to go,
Willing to serve,
Giving my all,
Holding nothing in reserve.
Whether sharing the gospel
Or witnessing to the lost,
Here I am Lord,
You paid the cost.

Whatever the need,
Whatever the test,
Here I am Lord,
Giving only my best.
I'm ready to go,
Willing to serve,
Giving my all,
Holding nothing in reserve.

Isaiah 6:8 "Also I heard the voice of the Lord, saying,
Whom shall I send, and who will go for us? Then said I,
Here am I; send me."

JESUS, THE KING OF KINGS

When I was filled with guilt and sin,
He's the one who took me in.
When I was lost, he saved my soul
He's the one who made me whole.

When I was depressed and filled with doubt,
He increased my faith and brought me out.
When I was sad, depressed for years,
He came along, wiped away my tears.

He's the one to whom I go,
He's the one that loves me so,
Thus, the reason that I sing
Is for the joy that He brings.
Wherever I go, whatever I do
I'll praise Jesus, the King of kings.

Now I know, when I'm feeling low,
He's the one to whom I go.
Now I know, when things go wrong,
He's the one to keep me strong

He's the one to whom I go,
He's the one that loves me so,
Thus, the reason that I sing
Is for the joy that He brings.
Wherever I go, whatever I do,
I 'll praise Jesus, the King of kings.

Revelations 19:16 "And he hath on his vesture and on
his thigh a name written, KING OF KINGS AND LORD
OF LORDS."

LORD, I NEED YOU

Speak to me Lord, just quietly say
Tell me your will for my life I pray.
Speak to me Lord; whisper in my ear
The words of truth I need to hear.

Walk with me Lord; hold my hand;
Give me the courage I need to stand
Walk with me Lord; show me the way;
Guide my feet, less I stray.

Lord, I need you; I need you today!
Lord I need you to come this way.

Share with me Lord, your life your love,
Teach me to appreciate blessings from above.
Share with me Lord, your goodness your grace,
Thou I'm not worthy to look upon your face.

Speak to me Lord, that I may hear,
Walk with me Lord; take away my fear.
Share with me Lord, your loving grace,
For Lord, I want to stay in the race.

Lord, I need you; I need you today!
Lord I need you to come this way.

Psalms 7:1 "O Lord my God, in thee do I put my trust; save me from all them that persecute me, and deliver me."

LORD, I

Have mercy on me Lord,
A wretch undone;
Fallen short of your glory
I have a race to run.
Lord, I surrender,
What else can I do?
Humbly I avail
Myself to you

Take and use me,
As you will.
And Your Word,
Lord, I will fulfill.
Judge me not
Lord I pray
Give me another chance
I'll do it your way.

Lord, I confess,
Repent and believe,
Save my soul
And my fears relieve.
Take and use me,
As you will.
And Your Word,
Lord, I will fulfill.

Psalms 141:1 "Lord, I cry unto thee: make haste unto me; give ear unto my voice, when I cry unto thee."

LORD I'M WILLING

Regardless of the season,
Be it winter or spring
Lord I am willing
To do anything

I'm willing to go
Both far and near
Preaching and teaching
Who ever will hear

I'm willing to do
Whatever the deed
Just to ensure
We meet the need.

Regardless of the season,
Be it winter or spring
Lord I am willing
To do anything

I'm willing to walk,
To talk and smile;
I'm willing to serve
To go the extra mile

I'm willing to share,
To love and inspire;
I'm willing to give
Whatever you desire

Psalms 145:1 "I will extol thee; my God, O King; and I will bless thy name for ever and ever."

LORD, YOU'RE THE ONE

Oh dear Lord, here I stand
Come and lead me to the promise land.
With all the love you placed in me,
Let me hide myself in thee.

Lord, I'm yours; I'm standing tall
Hold my hand less I fall
Guide me Jesus through the night
Shine on me your perfect light

Lord, O Lord, You're the one
You're His only begotten Son
Lord, O Lord, You're the way
You're the one in whom I pray

Holy, Holy here I stand
Please dear Lord take my hand.
Come sweet Jesus show the way
Help me make it through the day

Jesus, Jesus, Hear my plea
Come my Lord set me free
Lord I'm holding to a rope
But I'm slowly loosing hope

Lord, O Lord, You're the one
You're His only begotten Son
Lord, O Lord, You're the way
You're the one in whom I pray

Thank you Lord for hearing me
Lord your truth has made me free
Praise God, you didn't delay
Now I know you are the way

Because of you, I can see.
You opened my eyes to victory
Because of you, I can hear.
I no longer walk in fear

Lord I praise your Holy name
Because of you, I'm not the same
I'm on my way; I'm heaven bound.
A friend in you, I have found.

Lord, O Lord, You're the one
You're His only begotten Son
Lord, O Lord, You're the way
You're the one in whom I pray

Psalms 115:1 "NOT UNTO us, O LORD, not unto us, but unto thy name give glory, for thy mercy, and for thy truth's sake."

NO BODY BUT YOU

No body but you, no body but you
O Lord, no body but you.
No body but you can see me through,
O Lord, no body but you.

When I'm in trouble and need a friend
You're the one who steps right in.
You always come to rescue me;
You're always there to set me free.
When I'm down to my last dime,
You step in right on time.
You provide me with what I need
And I don't even have to plead.
No body but you, no body but you
O Lord, no body but you.
No body but you can see me through,
O Lord, no body but you.

Even when I am feeling low
With no one to call and no place to go
You're always there to answer my call,
You will not let me to fall.
There is no one, no one like you,
That's always there to see me through.
No matter when, no matter where;
Jesus you are always there.
No body but you, no body but you
O Lord, no body but you.
No body but you can see me through,
O Lord, no body but you.

Psalms 16:1 "Preserve me O God, for in thee do I put my trust."

REST IN THE LORD

If I am to someday be at peace
If I am going to pass His test
If I am going to do His will
I must learn to quietly rest
Rest in the Lord,
Rest in the Lord
O my soul rest in the lord.

Constantly moving, but going nowhere,
Not even taking time to eat.
Striving always to lend a hand,
Hoping to sit at my Savior's feet.

Going where I am not called
Doing things I am not told to do;
Bringing about heartaches and pain,
Wondering why, I am going through.

If I am to someday be at peace
If I am going to pass His test
If I am going to do His will
I must learn to quietly rest
Rest in the Lord,
Rest in the Lord
O my soul rest in the lord.

Psalms 37:7 "Rest in the Lord, and wait patiently for him: fret not thyself because of him who prospereth in his way, because of the man who bringeth wicked devices to pass."

STEP

We have come to worship God
To praise and magnify His Holy name,
Stand on your feet; make a joyful noise
Open your mouth; don't be a shame.

Step out of your mess, Step out of your flesh,
Step in God and be a fresh
Step in faith; step in love
And Praise our Father in heaven above

Shake off fatigue; shake off sleep,
Get up every body stand on your feet!
Forget your worries; forget your cares,
Throw your problems in the air!

Forget your heartaches; forget your pain,
Lift your voices Praise His name!
Give Him glory, Give Him honor,
Open your mouth, don't be a shame.

Step out of your mess, Step out of your flesh,
Step in God and be a fresh
Step in faith; step in love
And Praise our Father in heaven above

Psalms 37:23 "The steps of a good man are ordered by
the LORD: and he delighteth in his way."

About The Author

Felix is a born again Christian, who is committed to serving the Lord. In addition to being a poet, he is a minister/teacher of the gospel and a motivational speaker. His poems, which are inspired by God, are written to encourage, uplift and warn any and every one who reads them. They are written in a clear, simple and straightforward manner. His goal is to make sure that they can be easily read and understood.

Felix is married to the former Violet Gregory. They have two lovely daughters, Latavia Shante and Jasmin Mone. He is a loving husband and a dedicated father, who believes as Joshua did: "As for me and my house, we will serve the Lord."